Sum

Team of Teams

by General Stanley McChrystal

: This is a quick read summary based on the book "Team of Teams" by General Stanley McChrystal

Note to Readers:

This is a Summary & Analysis of "Team of Teams" by General Stanley McChrystal. You are encouraged to buy the full version.

TABLE OF CONTENTS

OVERVIEW

Team of Teams: New Rules of Engagement for a Complex World by General Stanley McChrystal is a *New Your Times* bestselling book exploring a new organizational model designed to be adaptable in the emerging and unpredictable world created by communication technologies. The author uses his considerable experience as a commander of the Joint Special Operations Task Force in Iraq, as well as drawing on several well researched examples from the corporate world, to make an argument that vertical and compartmentalized organizations are no longer well situated to thrive in the contemporary environment. Instead, he offers a detailed look at how he and others successfully transformed the Task Force based on the principles of shared consciousness and empowered execution. This review offers a detailed summary of the main themes and arguments in the book, followed by an analysis.

Retired General McChrystal is largely credited with the death of Abu Musab al-Zarqawi in 2006, who was at that time the leader of Al-Qaeda in Iraq. At that time he was serving as the commander of the Joint Special Operations Task Force in Iraq. He has also served as Commander of the International Security Assistance Force and U.S. Forces in Afghanistan. He has gone on to found the consulting firm the McChrystal Group along with others from military, academic and civilian sectors. The firm advises organizations on the kinds of practices argued for in this book.

SUMMARY

PART I: THE PROTEUS PROBLEM

CHAPTER 1: SONS OF PROTEUS

In this chapter, the author outlines a general argument that top down authoritative organizational structures are ill adapted to the contemporary environment. He uses two illustrative cases from military history to demonstrate his point. First, the efforts of the Joint Special Operations Task Force to combat Al-Qaeda in Iraq (AQI) in the early 2000s. Second is the strategy used by British admiral Horatio Nelson against the Franco-Spanish fleet in 1805.

In Fall of 2004, an AQI cell met in a neighborhood known as El Amel to plan a suicide bombing attack. They met in a safe house that was once a family residence. Although this operation included only three young men who would detonate triggers, the planning included dozens of people throughout a carefully guarded network of information gathering and strategic planning. However, the mission itself was crafted by the men in this room who made autonomous decisions which allowed them to adapt to the immediate shifting circumstances.

Seven men entered sedans chosen to blend in with traffic. They wore civilian clothes but were laden with weapons and other tactical equipment. The moved towards their target, a celebration at a sewage plant that had recently commenced operation. The planned starting locations for the maneuver were blocked by other traffic so the unit adapted. When the cars were in position, a code word was given. One of the cars drove straight into the crowd and detonated his bomb. In the immediate chaos American troops arrived on the scene as mothers frantically searched for their children. Then a second car drove into the crowd aimed at the soldiers and also detonated. The remaining coalition forces fired into a third oncoming car, causing it to detonate south of its target. The fourth car, with the capacity to detonate any of the cars remotely should they fail to, disappeared into the traffic and left the scene. Within hours of the incident which killed 10 Americans and 35 Iraqi children. Within a few hours, video of the scene taken by the men in the fourth car was posted online to be used for recruitment.

McChrystal was in charge of the Task Force during the time of the sewage plant bombing. The Task Force itself had been formed after the failed hostage liberation during the Iran hostage crisis in 1980. With forty years of experience, the most elite commanders and soldiers of the coalition forces, and access to the best in military technology, the Task Force was arguably the best and most accomplished Special Forces team in history. However, they were failing against a relatively underfunded group using outdated technology and poorly trained soldiers. In fact, attacks such as that on the sewage plant crowd were increasing in frequency. The Task Force was losing.

The author argues that it became clear that a new environment, one that would affect both military strategy as well as business models, had emerged. It was this new environment, information dense and rapidly evolving, that made the decentralized decision making structure of AQI so effective. Transforming the Task Force towards a new model of operation went against centuries of military tradition that emphasized top down authoritative decision making as the hallmark of efficient operations. The rest of this book will offer both step by step lessons learned in this process that have applications beyond military environments as well the subsequent research the author and his team did to test their organizational models.

The author then takes a bit of a detour to discuss the history of Abu Masab al-Zarqawi. As a teenager he was involved in drugs and alcohol and his mother sent him to a Salafist mosque where he gained a passion for jihad. He returned to Amman and then was arrested and imprisoned for a plot against the state. He further radicalized in prison and was 33 years old when released from the Suwaqah prison in 1999, along with several followers he had gained there. He went to Pakistan where Al-Qaeda was being formed but instead formed his own group, Tawhid w'al-Jihad (TWJ), which moved to start a training operation in Afghanistan. The group was close to Al-Qaeda, and when the U.S. invaded, TWJ allied with the Sunni minority that lost power when Hussein was deposed. TWJ had several successful and deadly bombing attacks while allied forces tried to secure Baghdad.

Terrorist attacks in Iraq by 2003 outnumbered the rest of the world combined, and the death toll from such attacks reached 1,000 a month by 2006. Power outages and sewage plant failures combined with the violence from terrorists to make the city a living hell. By pitting the Sunnis and Shias against each other, and contributing to the chaos of the collapse of the Iraqi state, Zarqawi hoped to make conditions ripe for a caliphate. By 2004 Zarqawi had sworn allegiance to Osama bin Laden and AQI was established.

Meanwhile, the Task force attempted to understand the power through which Zarqawi had so successfully mobilized and organized a small group of extremists into a more broadly supported insurgency in the region. Old ways of understanding power such as geographical territory or the charisma of singular leaders to inspire seemed to be falling short of understanding this new environment. Instead of maps, whiteboards became tools towards understanding the networks and connections between people and places. The new structures that emerged looked very different from the top down and hierarchical organizational structure typical of military regimes. They were also far less predictable. The author argues this shift was more than the tactics of guerrilla warfare, rather an entirely new structure created by the context of a changed environment. Even taking out people they knew were key players seemed to have little to no impact on AQI operations. The author argues that the internet and social media has changed the environment in ways that have made organizational structures like AQI a more effective kind of organization.

The author takes another turn here to showcase the tactics used by British admiral Horatio Nelson against the French and

Spanish fleets in 1805. The admiral knew that his armada was significantly smaller than the Franco-Spanish fleet. Instead of following the traditional battle plan which included lining the ships up parallel to enemy lines, he positioned the perpendicular and drove them into the lines of his enemy, breaking them up and positioning his own ships to fire from the port and stern while the target ships were left largely helpless because of their orientation. The author argues that even more interesting was that Nelson empowered the captains of each ship to be fully empowered to make decisions and guide their own maneuvers during the battle, rather than utilizing battle maneuvers guided real time by a fleet commander. The battle was a strong victory for Admiral Nelson because he took advantage of the chaos he created for the enemy who could not effectively use the flag signaling system they relied upon due to the smoke created from close combat. Nelson's success was about more than the rules of engagement on that particular battle, argues the author. It was also about cultivating a military culture among his captains that included training competence in autonomous and strategic decision making during battle. McChrystal came to see a similar pattern in AQI organizational structures and their effectiveness against the top-down hierarchical organizational style of the Task Force.

CHAPTER 2: CLOCKWORK

In this chapter the author explores the idea of efficiency. He begins by discussing various military contexts in which efficiency is achieved through developing highly rigorous and specific standards for various processes. The Romans had trained their army with this knowledge, drilling soldiers relentlessly, setting up every camp in precisely the same manor, and instilling a standardization that made it much easier for men to successfully move to different units and rapidly acclimate. Further, such discipline allowed the Roman soldiers, and the many militaries built on the same logic, to hold their lines during wartime, which was the largest predictor of success in battle. Modern armies have used similar tactics to enforce conformity. The author shares that during his time serving in the Ranger Regiment the level of detail was so exacting that there were regulations on the very kind of knot used to attach a shovel to his gear in a precise location. Such conformity meant that in battle, the search for supplies was as efficient as possible even in times of great duress.

Shifting gears to the civilian environment, the author argues that growing commercial ventures beyond small shops as a part of the age of industrialization also required similar strategies for efficiency. He highlights here the work of Quaker Frederick Winslow Taylor, the man who invented the concept of scientific management techniques. Taylor measured each step involved in a manufacturing processes, breaking it down into a series of movements based on optimizing efficiency. Despite triggering labor disputes among workers that had come to understand their knowledge and expertise as valuable, no longer the case in Taylor's system, Taylor's methods soon became the standard in industry. His system cut labor costs dramatically and significantly saved on material costs through optimizing manufacturing processes. Key to the success of Taylorism was shaving small amounts of time from each process, making the process entirely manageable from the top so that designs could take efficiency into account at all levels.

At its core, Taylorism rendered a process entirely predictable and controllable.

Although techniques of standardization had long been a part of military operations, Taylor's ideas in manufacturing inspired even more reduction of processes along these lines. Wartime production of weaponry in both WWI and WWII were successful precisely because untrained workers could be quickly trained to work on assembly lines to fill the labor gap of soldiers that left production for war. The sheer power of manufacturing in America during those periods stunned the world. Meanwhile, Taylor and those that learned and espoused his views were busy transforming every sector of the economy towards the principles of scientific management.

So pervasive were Taylor's methods, the author argues, that there was a shift in the ethos of Americans in a general sense towards valuing efficiency, and abhorring waste, particularly in the first decades of the twentieth century. By the 1960's however, some of the luster of Taylor's ideas had worn off. Douglas McGregor, professor at MIT, offered a famous critique of Taylor's methods based on challenging the fundamental assumption in Taylor's principles that assumed workers were lazy and stupid and thus needed financial incentive and micromanagement to be best motivated and handled. McGregor argued that managers would be more successful by treating employees with the respect that human beings need and deserve. Despite some accommodations to how workers are treated, scientific management as an organizational guiding principle remains largely unchallenged. Most large organizations appear roughly as a pyramid, with strategic planning done by a few at the top of the organizational hierarchy, and execution done largely at the bottom by a large pool of largely deskilled labor. So pervasive is this kind of structure in modern lives, argues the author, that it has permeated the way we conceive of social structure.

The Task Force in Iraq in the early 2000's very much embodied these principles of efficiency as well. Equipment was precisely stored down to the location of specific items in a soldier's pack which enabled the deployment of troops at a moment's notice. Large scale equipment was serviced according to strict routines which kept failure at a very low rate. Overall, the Task Force was a well-oiled and highly functional machine. Operations, which included integrating units across national lines, had been completely synchronized. Such synchronization was inspired largely by the failure of a joint operation to rescue American hostages from the U.S. embassy in Tehran. Before the mission was fully underway, a midair collision between a Navy helicopter and an Air Force cargo plane was a humiliating and public failure. The Joint Special Operations Task Force, now twenty years later, was a result of that horrendous failure. By 2003, when McChrystal took command of the Task Force, it was a very efficient and well equipped war machine focused on taking out top Ba'athist leaders of the fallen Hussein government. AQI, the insurgency led by Zarqawi, had not yet clearly come into focus. However, by early 2004 it was, and it was increasingly apparent that the flexibility and efficiency of small teams organized around specific goals and surgical precision were the tactics that were most successful. In part, the technology of war at that time dictated that such tactics would make the most of the risks involved, allowing for surveillance and information gathering to have the maximum effect on planning strikes.

The operations generally followed a five stage plan: Find, Fix, Finish, Exploit, Analyze. Targets needed to be located, their position fixed in real time, the target would then be acquired and then any information they would offer would be gathered. Finally, the operation would be analyzed, and the process iterated again on a new target. In and of itself, there was nothing particularly novel about this kind of approach, particularly in the context of elite forces. However, what was new was the scale of such operations, the speed and frequency with which they were being carried out. Within months they were incredibly efficient, and yet, there were signs emerging that the strategy was not working towards victory on larger goals in the area. AQI, despite being undermanned, underfunded and vastly technologically inferior, was thriving.

CHAPTER 3: FROM COMPLICATED TO COMPLEX

In this chapter the author argues that the vast data now available from tracing internet habits, and the power of social media to impact public opinion based on events that cannot be predicted and controlled, makes the world a less predictable place, rather than more so. This complexity arises directly from such technologies that connect humans across oceans in real time. The Taylorist vision of predictability through creating precisely controlled units answerable to a higher authority is a recipe for failure in this new environment. Moreover, this increased complexity is not just showing up in modern warfare, but across many domains such as biotechnology and economics.

The author explores the work of mathematician, Edward Lorenz. Lorenz built computer models of weather systems in the hopes of locating the underlying order of weather systems for better prediction. One day while running some tests he ran a simulation from a point halfway through a previous run, using data from a printout. The data he used for the inputs this time were, however, rounded to the nearest three decimal places, while the computer stored and utilized out to six. What he discovered was that within days out, the computer detailed a vastly different weather system based on extraordinarily small differences in a starting point. Years later, his paper "Does the Flap of a Butterfly's Wings in Brazil Set Off a Tornado in Texas?" was the origin of the term "the butterfly affect."

Complex systems of all kinds are subject to the butterfly effect. Complex systems are characterized by a large number of networked elements that interact with each other. Ecosystems, biological systems, and large scale economies, among many other examples, exhibit such complexity. Being complex and being complicated are fundamentally different in important ways. A system such as an engine has many interacting parts, and is a complicated machine, but it is not complex as it is a deterministic system. It behaves in predictable and controllable ways. Complex systems lack these characteristics.

This kind of unpredictability is known to mathematicians as nonlinear change, and the formulas that help us make sense of such phenomenon, such as those that help make sense of the stock market, are called nonlinear functions.

Effectively, a characteristic of nonlinear systems is that a very minute change in input will create very large shifts in output that wildly diverge over relatively short periods. Inherent in such systems is unpredictability that results from the potentially infinite micro interactions that can never be measured and thus brought under control. For Taylor's form of scientific management to be a sound management strategy, they system has to be linear because precise relationships between input and output are foundational to the prediction and control of that management style. The battlefield in Iraq in 2004 was just such a complex system. This was not a war of geographical territory held by troops on the ground with fixed locations in a battle of strategy based on offensive and defensive maneuvers. This was a network of complex interactional elements that could not be predicted, and thus the enemy was proving impossible to defeat with the techniques that would have been powerful against an enemy in another technological and social environment. The environment in which AQI was operating was a complex system.

The rise of interdependence in global culture is a result of a convergence of factors including intertwined economies, internet, social media and increased mobility across many domains. In addition, the pace of interactions has increased dramatically. Speed has always been critical to both militaries and businesses, however, now the increments that make a difference are minutes or seconds rather than days. The same technologies that one would think are providing well-funded operations like the Task Force with tremendous advantages are also introducing nonlinearity to the environment by creating networked communications and mobility that increase complexity. A single social media viral propaganda piece could spark an AQI terrorist reaction on the other side of the country, along with having an unknown impact on recruitment efforts and retaliations.

Business efforts too are grappling with the consequences of nonlinearity created by social media. For example, the author discusses the case of musician Dave Carroll who spent nine months trying to deal with United Airlines customer service to get recourse after his guitar was broken by baggage handlers. After he posted a video where he made a song about his experience went viral, the stock price dropped 10 percent, forcing the company to make a very public amends.

The author reiterates his point that tools that were successful in a different age are no longer effective in this new era. Systems need to adapt to be successful. Economist Friedrich Hayek has argued that national economies are essentially complex due to the large numbers of interactions at work. As economies have globalized, some economists have argued that nonlinear disturbances are becoming increasingly likely, and potentially even more catastrophic. There is a lure, after centuries of successfully applying Newtonian linear models to solve complicated problems, to assume that enough data and computing power could reduce the unpredictable nature of complex systems. However, that is simply not the case because of the nature of these kinds of systems. Complexity defies prediction, and complexity is here to stay. Efforts to try to break systems down into their components and reducing them to a predictable machine is simply not a viable solution to this problem, argues the author. By 2004 in Iraq, it was apparent that no matter how efficient the Task Force was, the unpredictability of AQI strikes meant that even the fastest possible response time was too long. A systemic change, something more radical than continuing to work on the efficiency problem, was necessary.

CHAPTER 4: DOING THE RIGHT THING

In this chapter the author explores the concept of resilience as a new way to think about creating stability in complex systems. It is contrasted to a paradigm of predict and control through designing complicated systems to optimize predictability. The author argues that despite the efficiency and streamlined processes of the Task Force, AQI was displaying tremendous resilience in the new complex environment. In this chapter the author will also offer several examples of resilient systems and problem solving solutions that focus on building resilience over optimizing prediction and control.

The author refers to the work of Brian Walker and David Salt to define resilience as those systems which can retain function and structure despite disturbances. The author explores the changing philosophy of the Danish in response to catastrophic floods in 1953 and the early 1990's to contrast these two paradigms. In 1953 a confluence of weather phenomenon caused the dykes the Danish had built to swell, taking 1,800 lives and destroying entire towns. The response to the crisis was to build the Delta Works, a 40 year long building project hailed by engineers as a modern wonder. This massive collection of dams, surge barriers, and sluices has been effective against threats from the sea. However, in the early 1990's melting snow from the Swiss Alps and heavy rainfall created a flood from behind, causing the evacuation of a quarter of a million people, and hundreds of millions of dollars in property damage. In response to this flood, engineers in the Netherlands have shifted strategy with a new program called Room for Rivers that is transitioning away from the highly engineered waterways to accepting the need for rivers to flood and more effectively making use of land in the natural floodplains that result from seasonal and climactic unpredictability. The new focus is building resilient systems, rather than complex systems that are inherently more fragile and subject to catastrophic failure.

Walker and Salt argue that optimizing elements of complex systems to try to bring them under control actually undermines resilience by creating a system that becomes dependent on each component behaving as expected. Thus, each element of a complicated system can become a site of vulnerability. Resilient systems, by contrast, absorb unexpected fluctuations. This phenomenon is also described by John Doyle, engineer at Caltech, who uses language that mechanistic systems are rigid, and such rigidity creates a brittle and unresilient system. The work of Andrew Zolli contrasts robust with resilience, suggesting that robust systems can be built to withstand known threats, but resilient systems can regenerate in the face of damage. Resilience is created when elements in those systems are linked in such a way as to adapt to change and damage. The author argues that we need systems that are both robust and resilient.

Efficiency, the drive of many business models since Taylor, and military models since Rome, can directly operate against resilience if it comes at the cost of adaptability in new and volatile environments. In military culture for centuries top down hierarchical organization, and the disciplined following of exact orders by those at the bottom from those at the top was a means of optimizing efficiency. The very concept of rank, central to military culture, was operating against the effectiveness of the Task Force. Although communication speed was enabled by new technology, waiting on the decisions of higher ranking officials, and security protocols designed to keep communications private, were both working against adaptability. Both vertical and horizontal aspects of hierarchy were operating against the need to be highly adaptable. Recognizing there was a problem, McChrystal and others set about fixing the organizational structures to be more in line with developing adaptability and resilience. They had a model to work from, that of al-Zarqawi and the networked cells of the AQI.

PART II: FROM MANY, ONE

CHAPTER 5: FROM COMMAND TO TEAM

The author begins this chapter by reviewing two commercial aircraft failures, the first was the crash of United flight 173 in 1978, the second was US Airways flight 1549 in 2009. In the first case, the structure of command placed the captain of the plane in charge of all activities, stressing his focus to the point that even after handling all of the consequences of an initial minor equipment failure, he missed realizing that they were running out of fuel after circling approach three times. Captain Sullenberger of flight 1549, however, worked an organizational structure built on teams, allowing him to put his focus entirely on flying the plane, and in an emergency landing lasting less than four minutes from incident, was able to successfully land the plane in the Hudson with no loss of life.

In April 2009, Captain Richard Phillips of container ship *MV Maersk Alabama* was held hostage by Somali pirates as the *USS Bainbridge* and the *USS Halyburton* waited nearby. Three days after the start of the standoff, three Navy SEAL snipers, dropped under cover of darkness, waited on the deck of the *Bainbridge* until the perfect moment arrived to simultaneously fire the three head shots that would kill all three pirates in an instant, saving the life of Captain Phillips. The author points out that despite the ensuing news coverage that focused on the individual skills of these elite warriors, their success was born just as much of their ability to work as a team cultivated through rigorous training to develop those skills. The author reviews some of the details of SEALs training, making the case that it is the ability to thrive as a member of tightly coupled teams under duress, more than individual physical prowess or specific skill mastery, which is the hallmark of those that succeed at SEAL training.

The author details two structures. One is a command based structure, the other that of a team. In the command based structure, there is a leader and several followers that are essentially interchangeable and all rely on the leader for decision making. In the team, there are a host of complex interactions among team members and a network of trusting relationships that tie them together. In the BUD/S phase of SEAL training, such relationships begin in training since much of the training exercises are built around cooperating with team members that stay constant for the duration of the training, except for those members that quit. An example of the emphasis of teamwork in the BUD/S training system is that trainees are punished if they ever are caught traveling alone without a swim buddy by being forced to roll around in the surf and sand.

The degree to which members of these teams know each other increases the degree to which the team can anticipate and work together, as well as developing the adaptive potential for the team itself. By cultivating instincts about what other people in the team's subtle cues are, the ability for individuals to operate as a functioning and adaptive team is vastly improved. In a Taylor kind of system, efficiency of operations happens when the further down the hierarchy one gets, the less contextual knowledge people need to have about the work that they do. The operators on an assembly line need only knowledge of the part of the operation that is in front of them, and their work is best when they simply master that simple operation. Most military operations operate on the same principle for efficiency. However, training people to have a very narrow view of their job fundamentally disempowers their ability to make sound decisions in situations not predicted by the designers of the processes. Moreover, such organizational structures tend to distance the workers of the lower ends of the hierarchy from the goals of the organization as a whole.

In contrast, members of a team are empowered to make decisions based on the immediate situation and cues, and understand their role in working with the team towards everyone's combined benefit. They are invested in the outcome of the team, and trained to operate adaptively in concert with evolving team goals. Team members tuned into others on the team can make decisions that are informed by the changing situation, and the capacity of their teammates to adapt as well. Members also need a strong sense of commitment to the cause of the team and the larger systems it is embedded in, argues the author. The tough and unpleasant SEAL training in large part weeds out those that are just not committed enough to wanting to be a SEAL, thus self-selecting for committed team members.

The author then turns to the concept of emergence, a phenomenon where many small scale and low level interactions combine to make a larger complex pattern. An example offered by the author is the resulting pattern and complexity of an ant colony, which contrary to popular belief, does not result from the top down telepathic orders issued by the Queen. Instead, the order of an ant colony is built from the instinctual reactions to a variety of complex stimuli as well as millions of interactions between the ants themselves. Likewise, Adam Smith's conception of the way the invisible hand shapes economic behavior via the individual acts of people operating from their own self-interest serves as another example of the concept of emergence.

The crash of flight 173 happened amidst a rise in aircraft accidents and prompted an investigation that revealed that in a host of these accidents a breakdown in the teamwork of the crew was contributing to poor performance and resulted in a host of preventable mishaps and tragedies. For years, as the safety of aircraft decreased despite increases in the inherent safety of the technology itself, management had faced the problem with typical Taylorist optimizing: developing ever more complex and exacting protocol trees for responding to every conceivable contingency. The investigation that followed flight 173 revealed that such complicated and top down procedures were hampering flight crew's ability to respond in the moment and make sound decisions in a timely manner. The author argues that this was a classic case of valuing procedure over purpose, and efficiency over adaptability in organizational structures.

The problem with operating in complexity is that there are potentially infinite possible contingencies, and attempts to plan in advance for every possible contingency at some point reach an unmanageable and even counterproductive level of detail and micromanagement that operates against effectiveness in the face of unpredictable situations. In the late 1970s NASA joined the FAA to face the flight safety concerns, and recommended a shift in organization that would emphasize teambuilding among the different crewmembers, each team of crew members having some autonomy to make decisions over their domain of expertise. The result was known as Crew Resource Management (CRM) which was implemented by the early 1980s. It focused on making the different teams involved in flying a plane more horizontally communicative rather than vertically positioning the Captain as the top of a hierarchical decision making tree. Special training programs trained crews to value teamwork and cooperation and to develop the same kinds of shared purpose and team communication as is emphasized in SEAL training. Despite resistance from pilots, CRM did increase overall safety. After 185 lives were saved from a catastrophic engine failure and subsequent crash landing of United flight 232 in 1989 was credited to the CRM techniques employed by the crew, CRM was mandated by the FAA and safety has increased dramatically as a result. The author then briefly explores a similar example of a shift in the way that American medical establishments treat trauma, and the formation of EMS services.

CHAPTER 6: TEAM OF TEAMS

By the mid-2000s the Task Force had achieved excellent efficiency in dealing with events that could be planned in advance. The different forces of the SEALs, the Rangers and The Army Special forces, had developed strong teams and were trained to be adaptable, however, the larger structure of the Task Force in which they were embedded had a preference for the kinds of mechanical operations based on rehearsing contingency plans. Such training was suited best for events that built up over time with predictable outcomes such as a hostage crisis, or locating and taking out single targets. Further, the units were isolated from each other so the cooperation and teamwork skills between divisions was limited, dampening flexibility. Furthermore, such specialization created a compartmentalization effect verses broad situational adaptability among the elite forces.

The author then introduces the term MECE (mutually exclusive and collectively exhaustive) to describe a kind of organizational strategy that seeks to compartmentalize certain chains of command and tasks so that the entire terrain of work is covered, and not duplicated. This pattern of organization has both efficiency and specialization as core structural elements. However, these strengths come at the cost of being able to allow people in the system to improvise, or make adaptive choices in a changing situation. The author uses a sports team to show how specialization combined with some overlap in responsibility can create both efficiency and the power to adapt to a changing context as well as to develop trust and nonverbal communication amongst teammates.

The author offers as an example the tensions between operators of missions and the intelligence teams trained to comb through potential intelligence gathered on scene. Both the operators and analysts had little understanding of the other's conditions for work, and as a result there was some tensions between the groups. Operators had little training on what kinds of materials would be best to collect, how to best document them, and also a degree of resistance in terms of prioritizing intelligence handling. Analysts were resentful about poor quality of materials, and the delays between an operation and receiving materials. The lack of integration between the teams had become a choke point in the operations as a whole, and as McChrystal and others identified them, and they termed them "blinks."

Blinks existed between different kinds of units within the Task Force, as well as between the Task Force and partners such as the CIA, FBI, NSA and other military units that they coordinated with regularly. The physical separation of these units was part of the design of the compound, and justified as a security precaution, however, it ultimately bred distrust as well as hampering information sharing. Organizational procedures in the various branches created bottlenecks that slowed the processing and disseminating of very time sensitive intelligence. While the Task Force operational teams had learned to include highly functional and communicative team cohesion, these operating forces were embedded in a larger top down structure with rigid hierarchies, which ultimately was stifling adaptive potentials.

Many organizations, including in the corporate world, have embraced team models to some extent. The author offers research data from Paul Osterman, an MIT economist, that among seven hundred manufacturers, most were using teams. Workplace studies more broadly have identified that teams lead to increases in productivity and morale. However, argues the author, adaptability is limited to the scope of teams. If the teams themselves are isolated in a larger culture of compartmentalization, then the benefits are limited. In addition, since the benefit of teams lies in the kinds of interpersonal cohesion of small groups, what does it mean to scale up this kind of operation across several thousand employees?

Although the context will determine the ideal size of teams, much beyond 30-40 people seems to stretch the ability to develop the sought for "oneness" that leads to adaptability beyond its natural capacity. However, the leadership in the Task Force came up with a novel solution: a team of teams. However, what McChrystal found was that individuals only needed to have tightknit relationships with other members of their team, but that the relationships between the teams needed to parallel the kind of structure as those between members of any one team. What they discovered was that if each person knew one other person from the other teams, it would help them envision a friendly face rather than a rival when working with the other teams.

PART III: SHARING

CHAPTER 7: SEEING THE SYSTEM

Security interests have contributed to the ever increasing and compartmentalization of information and the author argues in this chapter that it has compromised effectiveness overall. Controlling information has become more of the focus for handling information than sharing it in ways that best serve overall effectiveness. In order for operations in complex and rapidly evolving environments to be successful, a holistic view facilitated by as much up to the minute intelligence by those involved at the level of operations is critical. The author users a metaphor of a fictional soccer team to demonstrate his point. This team trains its players in isolation, developing a fantastic level of skills that the individual needs. In addition, the players wear blinders so that they can only see the parts of the field that are relevant to the kinds of plays their position would make. The problem is, despite incredible focus and outstanding personal skillsets, this team is beaten repeatedly by a team with much lower individual skills, but with the capacity to see the entire field as the game plays out.

The author offers another detailed example of the benefits of designing organizations based on a model of sharing information across specialties, and with a general of the system as a whole to be foundational to the leadership of individual teams. Prior to 1963, NASA's efforts to put a man on the moon were out of reach and largely considered by many to be a pipe dream given the current state of affairs and several embarrassing failures they had experienced to date. Leadership change in 1963, however, changed the organizational style of the organization and forced different specialties to come together and develop a holistic view of the entire process, rapidly transforming the organization culminating in successfully putting a man on the moon six years later. Changes were originally resisted, and it took discipline and dedication to maintain the kinds of interdepartmental communication that had become a successful model for designing a complex system. The organizational success of NASA, called systems management, was later used as a model for the construction of other complicated and high tech machines such as aircraft and the International Space Station.

Creating a team of teams for the Task Force would draw on these institutional successes and develop a more team oriented systems approach to its overall organization. While specialization clearly still had its place in terms of overall effectiveness and capacity to accomplish the mission, there was too much insulation between the different units to make the most of up to the minute intelligence of the evolving threat landscape.

Chapter 8: Brains Out of the Footlocker

In July 2004 the Task Force headquarters in Iran were moved to the Balad Airbase and McChrystal seized the opportunity to set about changing the institutional culture. He wanted to cultivate more information sharing between the units, as well as train all of his men and women to have a more holistic view of the entire operation. One of the first changes was to think through the physical layout of space and disrupt the usual military standard of segregating different kinds of units to reflect hierarchical structures.

The author argues that we tend to organize around behavior expectations, but the organization of space also encourages certain kinds of interactions. At Balad they wanted to design a physical space that encouraged the kind of networked organizational patterns that they wanted to become the new standard for operations. They used some successful models from the corporate world. In 1941, Bell Labs added common spaces such as a cafeteria to encourage interaction between departments. Google and other Silicon Valley corporations have been using open models of office layout as well as desegregating levels of management to great success to encourage collaboration and team spirit. At Balad the main bunker was opened up into the Joint Operations Center (JOC) which was a massive open space as the central nervous system of operations. A large table was set before screens displaying real time information and video from various live operations and surveillance and leaders from all of the teams spent a good deal of time operating from this central location, sharing their different perspectives on the stream of data. Other tables were also set up in this space so that all of the functional teams of the entire Task Force had access and input in live time. Anyone was empowered to grab a microphone and address the entire JOC at any time if they had germane information or perspective. The JOC was focused on operations in Iraq. McChrystal also created a Situational Awareness Room (SAR) with a similar design, but the focus was more on the shifting environment of Al Qaeda's activity on a global scale.

The change in the layout of command operations was not going to be enough, but it was a start. The Task Force needed to refine its organizational structure by shifting the culture. McChrystal wanted to create a kind of shared and emergent consciousness, but this ran counter to decades of culture based on carefully guarding information and strong rivalry among different branches. The Operations and Intelligence brief (O&I) was a daily meeting with the top intelligence and command officials. When McChrystal took over command, he grew the audience for the O&I so that more people could participate in this vital exchange of information on operations. In addition, they invested in increasing bandwidth vital for secure communications to enhance the network of communication on a variety of intelligence.

There was resistance by many to this new system at first. Since much of the resistance came from the cloistered intelligence communities, McChrystal made sure to improve the kinds of real time access to raw intelligence as a way of showing generosity. As time wore on however, it became more and more clear that increased sharing of information was benefitting overall effectiveness, creating more of a draw towards open communications. Another deliberate effort was to have operators and analysis work together, which helped to both foster trust between the two units, but also improved intelligence gathering and sharing as more understanding of the context in which the other group was operating helped to refine both processes. Although perceived as redundant from the older standards based on a MECE kind of structure, what began to emerge from the interactional O&I meetings was a greater general understanding of the complexity of the environment.

One critique of information sharing has stemmed from wikileaks incidents by people such as Edward Snowden and Bradley Manning. Such information leaks have compromised national security interests, concedes the author. However, he also argues that the overall gains of information sharing have far outweighed the offsets, and that security measures that do not compromise information sharing efforts can still be put in

place to minimize the risks of security breaches.

Chapter 9: Beating the Prisoner's Dilemma

The author begins this chapter by reviewing the classic game theory problem of The Prisoner's Dilemma as a way to introduce the problem of developing trust among the various groups at the Task Force. In this story two people are arrested for a crime and told that if they rat on their partner, they will receive no jail time, but in return, their partner in crime will receive two years. If both betray the other, then both will end up serving two years. However, if both stay silent, they will each only serve on year. Although there is a chance that one could serve no time if they rat and the other does not, the total time served would be the two years served by the other. The moral of this story is that if the criminals can trust each other to be silent, it is likely by both staying silent the best overall solution to the dilemma is found, although it requires putting the combined benefit over the individual benefit.

Competition has long been a part of the intelligence and military communities, and has long been considered as a healthy rivalry that encourages people to do their best work. However, the author argues that it also fosters hostility and reluctance to share. New ways of doing things would need to incentivize sharing. In particular, knowing that everyone sharing would help overall effectiveness was not enough to overcome the barriers of trust that if one branch shared information the others would reciprocate. The knowledge is power paradigm, forged in a competitive environment, was entrenched. Fundamentally, trust building across the different units was a priority.

One successful, if controversial, program was to embed people in units outside of their own training expertise. Initial resistance was based on endless explanations of how each unit has fundamentally different training systems and that such embedding would be disruptive of the team cohesiveness that such training was designed to achieve. However, when forced, the candidates selected for the embedding were the top, due to the pride factor of each unit wanting to show their best to the other units. Many of these candidates happened to also have good teamwork qualities, so the results ended up being very successful. The end result was that a mutual respect for the different unit's strengths due to different training styles, resulted. In addition, the embedded operator was seen as a representative of their unit, and thus helped to foster inter-unit respect across the board, fostering a willingness to cooperate. In addition, the role of liaisons to partner ambassadors, previously selected among some of the near retirement and often burned out officers to get them out of the battlefield, was shifted to selecting some of the best field tested and ambitious commanders. This greatly strengthened important institutional ties to distant networks in this new global and complex terrain. The result was better information sharing, and more robust alliances, strengthening the network at hubs where it had previously been allowed to atrophy. By developing stronger relationships with distant nodes of operations, and by backing them up by empowering these liaisons to share resources and intelligence, the nodes were significantly strengthened. Many of the partner organizations reciprocated by sending their own liaisons to the Task Force SAR.

Sometimes emerging intelligence meant that a unit that was assembling for a mission might suddenly have to stand down as the intelligence shifted and another mission took priority and thus received access to helicopters and other essential but limited mission critical technology. Prior to the information sharing, such assets were considered in a vacuum where they were just "lost" to another team, fueling a sense of competition and hostility. However, when such teams were brought in on the intelligence that informed such decisions, they were able to see how the larger goals in the region were being served best by such shifts due to up to the minute intelligence, changing the kinds of meaning they made about losing assets to other teams for higher priority missions suddenly cleared by emergent intelligence.

The author offers an example by way of detailing the kind of mission that demonstrates the increased effectiveness of such a focused and cooperative effort across divisional lines.

The incident begins moments after an empowered analyst sees activity near a location recently targeted. Within moments operators are in the air, with real time updates of potential interception points along the target vehicle's route. Before they arrived at the target, it met another vehicle and exchanged a person, and now two target vehicles speed off in opposite directions. The team split to follow both assets. As soon as an operator interrogated the first vehicle on the scene they confirmed that a high level target was in the second vehicle, allowing a rapid shift in resources to that vehicle which successfully captured the high value target. Such split second plan adaptation required real time coordination and willing and enthusiastic teamwork among several units within the Task Force and is exemplary of the kinds of mission level gains that such organizational structures can achieve.

The author then turns to the case of GM where he traces organizational culture over the span of a century to shed light on a 2014 congressional investigation on why it took 12 years to diagnose and repair a faulty ignition switch issue that simultaneously cut the engine off and disabled airbags with relatively little pressure on the ignition switch in the Chevy Cobalt and Pontiac G5. In 1918 Alfred P. Sloan joined GM as an executive and found a company in turmoil from a slew of recent acquisitions and chaotic organizational structure that had started to severely compromise profits. His efforts to establish order included a MECE style of organizational management, which was at the time rather controversial. However, the design was very effective, reduced redundancy, and its success became the justification for what would become the corporate standard through most of the twentieth century. However, by the 1970s the system started showing problems. The same silos created by the MECE structure showed an inability to adapt to changing U.S. consumer preferences, and competition with Japanese car manufacturers. The author argues that these issues remained largely unaddressed by 2002 when the ignition switch issue first came to light because the technical issue of the switch lay between two deeply compartmentalized departments who were territorial and non-cooperative. The fact that it took 12 years to finally address the problem, after costing the lives of at least 13 people, is a result of the failure of the MECE model in the complex environment of today's markets and technology, argues the author. The author details a shift away from the MECE model towards a more integrated approach at Ford in 2005 under the leadership of Alan Mulally. He credits this shift towards a model predicated on sharing information and transcending departmental silos as the factor that allowed Ford to survive the 2008 financial crisis without filing for bankruptcy.

The work of Sandy Pentland, professor at MIT, confirms that the collective intelligence of a well networked group of people is much greater than the sum of its parts. Flow of ideas is essential towards building this kind of collective intelligence. His work shows that both engagement between different teams, as well as focusing on exploring common problems, helps most to foster growth towards a more integrated operation. The author argues that although operationalizing such systems for the Task Force was originally met with opposition, the overall effectiveness gained

outweighed losses in efficiency at the lower levels as well some

increased risk of potential information breeches.

PART IV: LETTING GO

CHAPTER 10: HANDS OFF

As the transition to a more teams based approach started to take shape for the Task Force, McChrystal realized that there was still a bottleneck in terms of the various approvals through the chain of command that had to take place before a mission was approved, significantly decreasing time to mobilization. The author equates the situation to a soccer team that has to get written permission before passing the ball during a game. Moreover, the people higher in the chain of command often had less direct information about the rapidly shifting environment than the operators and analysts closer to the operation.

The author then uses an historical example to demonstrate styles of leadership in military environments. Commodore Matthew Calbraith Perry was sent by the U.S. Navy with extraordinary latitude in the methods that he would use to secure a trade agreement with Japan in 1852. In contrast, Ulysses S. Grant gave very detailed instructions during the same time period as to the exact movements of troops in the Army, even going so far as to mandate very specific budget orders such as growing rather than buying vegetables for the troops. The author argues that the difference in culture mainly resulted from the fact that there was no ability to communicate with ships far off at sea. Typically, the more capacity for communication, the more military organizations tend to favor top down micromanagement.

The author argues that in a complex environment such as the modern battlefield, the drive towards centralization has outlived its purpose. Rather than creating a sense of order and decisions made from the position of best knowledge, now over-centralized command runs the risk of making decisions with less contextual information, and slowing decision making to the point that it compromises effectiveness. As a result, McChrystal began to rethink his own role as a leader. He changed the command structure so those below him in the command chain were more empowered to make decisions to go on a mission that met certain criteria.

Decentralization of decision making, also known in business theory as "empowerment," has been a well-studied approach to managing employees. Research across a wide variety of national and employment sector domains demonstrates that empowerment improves employee morale and motivation. Meanwhile, the modern complex environment has caused micromanagement techniques to skyrocket in terms of cost. This is due to the complexity of new environments. There are too many emergent possibilities for top down decision making to be effective at keeping companies flexible and innovative enough to thrive if they try to plan for every conceivable contingency. For example, had a service representative with United been more empowered help Carroll with his broken guitar, the massive public relations scandal that required a public apology after stocks dropped in response to his viral video may have been avoided.

Over time a general rule of thumb emerged to guide subordinate officers to authorize missions. A mission needed to serve overall goals in the region and needed to be both moral and legally sound. The shift marked a dramatic increase in effectiveness. The author explains that when people make decisions, they become more personally invested in the success of the outcome. Empowering people to make decisions at various levels of an organization can have a profound impact on how devoted they are to the overall goals of the operations, in either business or military environments. What happened as a result of empowered decision making, the author argues, could not have happened without the foundation of shared consciousness detailed in previous chapters. The amount of real time access that McChrystal had to ongoing operations was unprecedented. From his laptop he could tune in to the communications of live events, as well as observe video feeds and satellite imagery. He had to allow other competent people to make the kinds of in the moment decisions that their training and presence on the ground best situated them to do. The number of raids that the team was successfully operating went from 18 to 300 per month, with higher success rates overall.

CHAPTER 11: LEADING LIKE A GARDENER

In this chapter the author reflects on our cultural stories about good leaders, and argues that we need to amend our picture of strong leadership to allow organizations to take on new shapes and thrive in complex environments. Some have made the mistake of understanding empowered execution such as that described in the previous chapter as a leaderless system. For example, many have argued that the network like structure of AQI and other terrorist organizations is essentially leaderless. However, the author argues this is a mistake. There is more need than ever for sound leadership, it just necessarily looks different than leadership in centralized command structures.

Leaders in modern complex environments are responsible for cultivating effective culture. No one person can master the entire field because the sheer complexity of the modern environment and the colossal amount of data that we can generate about it, be it markets or battlefields, is simply too much for any one person to be empowered to see the system with a God's eye view. Emergent collective consciousness is required for organizations to make the best use of their employees and soldiers. The author uses the metaphor of a garden to demonstrate this management approach. The initial planning is important, but what is more important than deciding where each plant will go is the constant tending, weeding and maintenance that keeps a garden thriving. Successful gardening is about providing an environment for the plants to thrive. McChrystal used his authority to cultivate the high levels of transparency and information sharing that successfully transformed Task Force operations.

One of the tools that McChrystal used to great success was writing daily emails that targeted a large number of people in every unit to be sure that his voice permeated the noise of information flow. He kept his words short, but meaningful, and they were designed to give guidance on priorities and the expectations of the new culture. He sought to convey a consistent message and set an example of transparency. In addition, coordinated daily teleconferences with the force via the O&I sessions was an important opportunity for cultivating the kind of environment where people could develop a holistic understanding of operations and their role in the larger context. Fostering active interaction at the O&I was an important priority for McChrystal. The O&I also included reports from the field from much less senior officers and operators, giving them an opportunity to know that their input was valued. In addition, McChrystal asked questions to allow others to show their expertise to the thousands that were in attendance at the O&I meetings. The leader of organizations determined to grapple with complexity, reiterates the author, needs to be able to give up control to those around him and take on the role of a person that cultivates a successful environment that empowers other competent people to make decisions from their locations.

PART V: LOOKING AHEAD

CHAPTER 12: SYMMETRIES

The author begins this chapter with a description of the events leading up to the death of al-Zarqawi, highlighting the ways in which their new method of operations contributed significantly to their success in the operation. First they captured an asset who gave them intelligence on the location of a spiritual advisor, Sheikh Abd al-Rahman, who was known to have regular visits with Zarqawi. By pooling assets from across the region, and by the cooperative nature of the various units, the Task Force was able to track Rahman with nonstop surveillance for several days. When he departed the city, he swapped vehicles several times, and entered and exited a restaurant to try to throw off anyone on his trail. At each swap the team was able to run simultaneous surveillance on all of the vehicles in case of a ruse. Finally, Rahman came to a large mansion and Zarqawi himself came out to greet him, providing the visual confirmation of his presence. Despite having some hurdles with equipment, the Task Force was able to mobilize F-16 bombers to bomb the residence. Although Zarqawi exited the building alive on a stretcher, he died within a half an hour of the strike. None the less, his capture was a major victory which marked a turning point in the battle against AQI.

By 2006 the Task Force had become a highly effective and adaptable team. By combining decentralized leadership and radical transparency, the team was both robust and adaptable. The fight against AQI was turning to the advantage of America and its allies. They were able to strike nodes of the AQI network faster than they were able to reassemble and regenerate.

In the final paragraphs of this chapter, the author considers the changes to human behavior and organizations that will necessarily continue to happen as we confront the complexity of modern life. He argues that the models that have been very successful at solving problems in the past are no longer relevant and that new and emergent solutions are what we need to be seeking out. The mechanistic world view that was so very important for industrialization at the start of modernity is now becoming obsolete. We need to build systems capable of adapting to emergent phenomenon in chaotic environments.

ANALYSIS

This book is likely to have wide appeal among leaders across a wide variety of sectors from the military to nonprofits. McChrystal successfully communicates his passion for transforming organizations to thrive in modern environments full of unpredictability and complexity. His arguments are compelling and well laid out. The examples he draws from add color to the narrative, but stay relevant to the developing articulation of first the problem and then the solution. In addition, since he draws from both military and corporate history, there is credibility built throughout the book that the ideas he shares in this book have a wide range of applications.

McChrystal is particularly adept at describing theoretical concepts such as nonlinear complexity in ways that are accessible to the reader. Many readers will have no trouble relating to the evidence provided that the world today is profoundly different from the twentieth centuries in ways that are thrilling and frightening. Moreover, the author's liberal use of examples from historical cases demonstrates that the same organizational structures that once thrived are losing relevance.

At times the author is repetitive of some of the key themes in ways that disrupt the flow of the narrative. For example, despite having made the point in the first few chapters that top-down, MECE styles of organization lack the adaptability necessary for the modern environment, the point is remade several times throughout the book. Similarly themes of interdependence, emergence, shared consciousness, and unpredictability are repeated frequently throughout the text. As a result, there are moments when the author comes off as a bit preachy. Another disappointment of the book is the lack of academic work from the fields of business and management that would have leant more credibility to some of the author's claims. While some research is used in the book, it is not as well sourced as it could be in terms of drawing on the substantial body of scholarship concerning organizational theory.

While strong on theoretical clarity, the book does suffer somewhat from a lack of implementable guidelines. Part of that is likely deliberate, as the author would probably argue that context will have to determine many of the specific organizational structures that work best. However, some readers will certainly wish for more in the way of pragmatic guidelines. However, the lack of practical suggestions does not draw away from the inspiration that many will take from this book. It is certainly a worthwhile read for anyone interested in topics concerning leadership and organizational theory.

49868376R00042

Made in the USA
Lexington, KY
24 August 2019